when
the stars
collide

Stay a little longer under the moonlit night and
admire the diamond, star-filled sky.
Gaze into the abyss where time no longer exists.

MELINA S. FARAHMAND

when
the stars
collide

Book Cover, Typesetting and Interior Book
Design by Anamaria Stefan

Illustrators: Alyssa Neumann and
Yasmin Atienza

content

"The nitrogen in our DNA, the calcium in our teeth, the iron in our blood, the carbon in our apple pies were made in the interiors of collapsing stars. We are made of starstuff."

— Carl Sagan, Cosmos

*Dedicated to the children
of the cosmos who still
believe in magic.*

Author's note:

Hi humans. I hope you're all doing well. After
publishing my debut book, "From Dust to Breath,"
I mainly focused on journalistic writing and wanted
to wait for inspiration to strike before working on
my second book. During the pandemic, I decided
to challenge myself to try some different things
with this newfound time. Besides learning to make
beignets and many other desserts, I was reminded
of my love for poetry back from my elementary
school days. I haven't written poetry in YEARS.
While I don't consider myself a poet per se, I am
a writer at heart, and as a writer, it's essential to
challenge yourself to create pieces outside of your
comfort zone in styles you may not always practice
in. The work I've done in the past came naturally
and effortlessly; however, I wanted to push myself
to write in a format that I haven't written in for a
very long time and in a form that entails a bit more
thinking.

I want to clarify that this book is not merely poetry. I'd even go as far as to say that this is not a poetry book. Not all of the pieces in this work are in typical poetic form or use poetic devices. Don't go into this book looking for a Shakespearian style of writing. The best way to describe the pieces you are about to read is that they're a compilation of mantras, thoughts (many of which are philosophically influenced), ideas, messages, and a poem or two (or three), haha. I hope you enjoy reading this book. It was a lot of fun to dive into the cosmos to search for magic, learn more about life/death, remembering to lead with love, and empower the human soul.

I hope you enjoy reading these pieces, and more importantly, I hope, like my first book, that they make you reflect more profoundly about the life you want to live. Through the dark and the light, I hope you live one remarkable, adventure-filled life.

chapter 1

STELLAR COLLISION

"A stellar collision is the coming together of two stars caused by stellar dynamics within a star cluster, or by the orbital decay of a binary star due to stellar mass loss or gravitational radiation, or by other mechanisms not yet well understood."

Golden girl made of storm clouds, sunshine, and rain.
Golden boy made of heartache, love poems, and pain.

'*Let's party and live like it's our last day on earth,*'
says the young at heart;

'*Keep going, you've got so much left to live for,*'
says the old soul;

'*I'm tired, and I want to go home*'
says the broken heart.

We don't have all the *time* in the world to accomplish our dreams; we must do what we can now. *Dreams*, like the sands in an hourglass, eventually run out.

I'll see you in the next life, *my friend.*
This one alone is simply not enough. If I get there
first, *I'll save you* a seat next to me so we can
reminisce about all the dreams we once shared and the
love we couldn't quite repair.

Some people will always have a *special* place in your *heart*, even if they can no longer hold a special place in your *life*.

I have been down this road before, my friend, and I
know the way out— so take my hand, and I'll lead
you on the path back home.

There will always be a part of me that will *believe* in the good of *humanity* and the *beauty* of *humankind*, despite evidence to the contrary.

Always and forever, *my friend*, always and forever,
well... at least until forever ends.
And when the time comes for us to say our last goodbyes, I
will *hold you in my arms* tightly while the light
of the stars shine on us brightly
Until we must go our separate ways.
But just know deep in *your heart* that those
who *love* deeply and unconditionally will always
be together in life and in death. We will remain
connected beyond the depths of the Earth and will be so
until the end of time, *always and forever.*

Before I die, tell me that I was a good
human being. Tell me that *I made a
difference in people's lives.*
Make me believe that all the pains of my
existence were worth it.

There are certain *words* we will *never forget*, no matter how many apologies are said. They are stuck like dead flies in the web of our *memory*.

Stop using toxic people to fill up your loneliness. It's better to be happy and alone than to be with evil people who are poison to your soul.

Welcome to the
club of *broken
hearts*;
we've been
expecting *you*.

And it turned out that the misunderstood heroine, ridiculed for her strength and bravery, was the *heroine* every little girl needed growing up. So, like any good *superhero*, she rose above the spiteful rhetoric and carved her own path.

Here's to the lonely and broken-hearted; we
raise a glass to ones who try their hardest, to the
do-gooders, peacemakers, and lovers alike—a
toast for the ones who are pure of heart.

Even the most *beautiful angels* must battle the most hideous demons within.

To the *moon* for always being there on the darkest of nights. To the *sun*, for continuing to shine bright. To the *stars*, we've wished upon. To the cosmos and the unknown they hold. We give you our heartfelt thanks. You've given us wings for our wildest dreams so we can soar through the *heavens* and the skies, looking for life's next adventure.

It has been an honor of a lifetime to have walked this earth with you. If only we could punch our ticket one more time and begin our journey anew.

chapter 2

SUPERNOVA

A star that suddenly increases greatly in brightness because of a catastrophic explosion that ejects most of its mass.

/ˌso͞opərˈnōvə/

noun ASTRONOMY
noun: **supernova**; plural

noun: **supernovae**; plural
noun: **supernovas**

When the *lights* come down, and it's all said
and done, I can only *hope* that I'm remembered
more for the things I did, rather than only the
things I said. The change enacted, the lives
impacted. May history remember me as the girl
who acted and made the *world* a better place.

Fight for the *soul* of humanity and the *heart* of mankind. Look evil in the eye, and hold your gaze until he bursts from your fiery flames.

Don't let fear kill your *dreams* before they can even sprout their roots. Stare it in the eye like a bully, until it blinks, shrinks, and slips away.

There were two rules my diving instructor taught me before my first dive: *never stop breathing* and don't come up too fast. Don't be like the guy on the train from New York to California who never once opened his shade.

I hope you find the courage within yourself to be everything you were meant to be. Live to your fullest and *you'll always be free.*

You're still here. Despite everything, you are still here. And every day, the sun will rise, and you shall carry on like the soldier you were meant to be. A kind soul with the strength and heart of a warrior, you will carry on.

Standing on the balcony, drink in hand, she basks
in the New York City lights, and dreams of a plan to
conquer the world.

Be the *rainbow* when the rain is still falling.
Be the *beam* of sunlight streaming through
the dark clouds on a stormy day.
Be the *hope* where there's only despair.
Be the *light* in the world.

Child of the cosmos made of stardust,
chaos, and all the galaxies combined. Your mighty
soul reaches all the corners of the universe.
From the beginning of time till forever.

Be the hero the younger version of yourself
needed growing up. Wear your invisible cape
proudly like a badge of honor and save yourself
from the depths of self-destruction.

Each of us will have our final curtain call,
make sure the show that comes before is
worth the price of admission.

Storytelling gives us a chance to have things go our way for once. We can create our own *beginning*, write our own *happy ending*, and through our characters, live the life we always dreamed we could.

An *ode* to the *stories* and characters
who made us who we are—*a song* of
praise to the ones who'll always have a
special place in *our hearts*.

We believed we could, so we did.
We were the crazy greater fools who took the risk.
Head first. Feet last.
We stood on the edge of the horizon, sunlight
shining on our faces, and we dove right into the deep end.
Be the greater fool and take the risk.

If you have a story to tell, do whatever you have to do to make sure it's heard. Shout from the rooftops, scream it in the streets, just don't leave it on the page.

Be a guardian of your democracy,
a custodian of your planet, and
a marvelous child of the cosmos.

chapter 3

FROM THE REMNANTS, A NEW STAR WILL ARISE.

Like a *Phoenix*, continue to
rise from beneath the ashes,
with the magic that lies within
and take that *power* to shatter
every glass ceiling and create healing
Within a nation that is too busy
grieving instead of dreaming,
we are pleading with you
To rise into the fire-filled sky
with your wings created by kings —
Rise like the *Phoenix*, trailblazer.

For we can be so much more
If only we dared to hope,
dared to dream, dared to believe
That we can be all that we need
If only we just take the leap
And ignite the revolution that lies in our
souls to set the world on fire
So we can burn brighter than ever before
Brighter than we ever thought we could.

We did what we could with what we had.
We left everything on the battlefield. All the blood,
tears, triumphs, and losses. We can hang our hats on
a life well lived with no regrets. So, in the end, we
can take our bow, and be proud.

Sometimes our best isn't good enough, and that's okay. We gather our *courage*, we gather our *hope*, and return to try another day. In hopes that the seeds we planted before will grow and soar above the ground when the time is right.

I fully intend to give this life everything I've got. I intend to give it my whole heart and if you lend me yours, I'll give that, too.

The fairytale was rewritten, and she was no
longer the *girl* who *fell in love* with
the *prince*; she was the damn *queen*,
and this queen didn't need anyone saving her.

Be a freakin trailblazer, darling. Shatter every glass ceiling. Raise your voice — shout if you must. Break down every barrier they've put to block your way. Be the pioneer who carves the path, not one who follows others' footsteps. Shine your light brightly and ignite the spark for others to be inspired then fan the flame. Be the heroine you needed as a child, and never settle for anything less.

The *power* of the *universe* lies within her; she will always *shine* brightly even on her darkest days, for she is made from the remnants of the *stars* and all the galaxies that have collided, sprinkling *magic* into her essence.

So you've been dealt cards that you don't like,
given a script that's not quite right, who's to
say you can't rearrange the deck or change the
story to better fit your life.

We were extraordinary people who let the ordinary convince us we were not. Slam the door in the face of the doubters and claim your highest self.

I want to shatter every *single glass* ceiling,
and use the shards to make history.

You've got *magic* in your *soul* and *fire* in your *veins*, there's not a thing on earth that can stop you once you hold the reins.

I cannot *control* the things that life throws my way, but I can control how I react to its *challenges*. Just like I can't control the winds of the sea, I can adjust my sails to continue the *journey*.

When we look beyond the limits we've
placed on ourselves, only then will we see
our potential to be all that we can.

May your *memories*
be a revolution to all who *remember you*
And may your life
be one glorious *adventure.*

chapter 4

CELESTIAL,
COSMIC LOVE

Positioned in or relating to the sky, or outer space as
observed in astronomy."a celestial body"

ce·les·tial

adjective /səˈlesCHəl/   adjective: **celestial**

Stay a little longer
under the *moonlit night*
and admire the diamond, star-filled sky.
Gaze into the abyss
where time no longer exists.

Don't kill your dreams before they even have
the chance to grow. So plant faith deep in your
heart, not fear in your mind. Embrace the
courage in your bones and fire in your soul. Let
your magic lead the way.

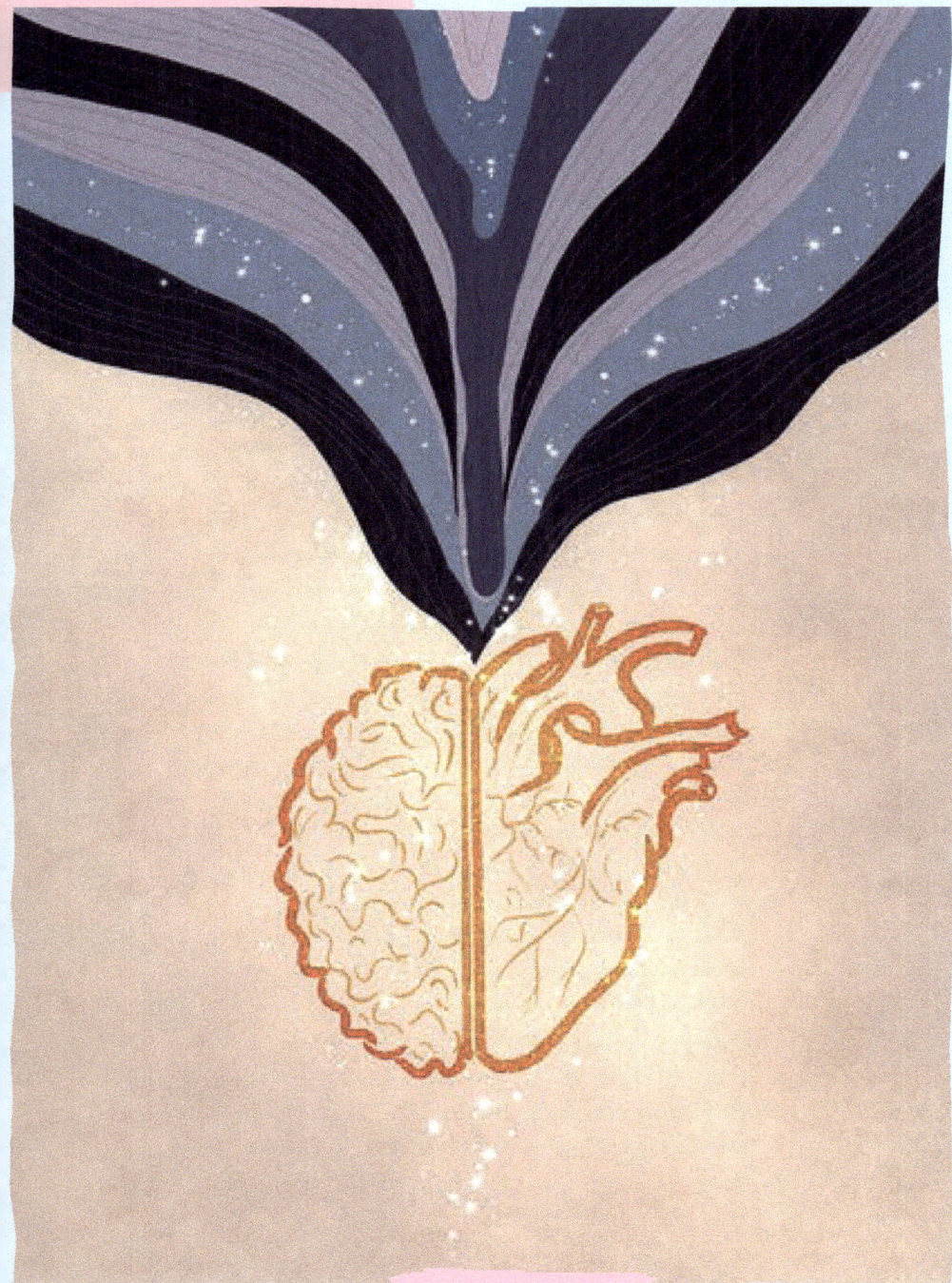

If you are willing to live life to the fullest, it will be worth every bleeding footprint, every *heartbreak* and sad day.

Let's chase some sunsets along the shoreline and *dance* under the *moonlight*. Feel the water on our toes and dream of the better days to come.

From the moment you make your grand
entrance into this world to your final bow,
your miraculous arrival to your heartfelt
departure, from the time you're dust to your
very first breath— make sure your life story
is one worth remembering.

My psychology teacher used to say that, 'we can look at your brain, but we can't look inside your mind.' And I think the same applies to the human heart— we can see it, touch it, fix it and stitch it up, but we can never look inside your soul.

It's you and I until the end of time. My heart
is yours and yours is mine.

I love you, wholeheartedly, unconditionally, and everlastingly. *I love you* like the sun loves the moon, and the sky loves the sea and more than all of the stars in the galaxy.

When it comes time for me to face the gates and glory above, I hope that I can look back with pride, knowing I've done everything I was meant to do, used every gift I was given, lived life fully, and created a legacy worth remembering.

One day we will meet again amongst
the stars, and we will talk about all the things we
once loved and all the things we wished we could
have done. I'll meet you in the world
in-between where nothing is what it truly seems.

As a young girl, I was *lucky* because I not only had princesses growing up. I also had generals who were tough but also soft, *superheroes* who saved the world, brilliant doctors who were career-driven, and lawyers who didn't take no for an answer. I had scientists who believed in the impossible and made it happen— I had women who showed me what *leadership, empathy, kindness*, and *intelligence* can do to make this world a better place.

Walk this earth with *love* in your *heart*, knowledge in your mind, and chaos in your bones. Squeeze life like a sponge until there's not a drop left.

Leaving behind
Everything that was
Golden and good
And deeply
Cherished for
Your loved ones to hold
in their hearts forever.

— *What is
a legacy?*

Ride the wave, darling. Ride the wave until you reach the shore and then run towards the light.

Once you learn to relinquish *hate* and retain *love*, you will see the *light* in the world, and you will feel that sparkle glimmer in your *heart*.

May you always be a *fearless child*
of the *cosmos*, rising through the heavens
on the *wings of love*.

Keep the
faith until
the end.

"The knowledge that the atoms that comprise life on earth — the atoms that make up the human body, are traceable to the crucibles that cooked light elements into heavy elements in their core under extreme temperatures and pressures. These stars— the high mass ones among them went unstable in their later years. They collapsed and then exploded, scattering their enriched guts across the galaxy. Guts made of carbon, nitrogen, oxygen, and all the fundamental ingredients of life itself. These ingredients become part of gas clouds that condense, collapse, form the next generation of solar systems— stars with orbiting planets. And those planets now have the ingredients for life itself. So that when I look up at the night sky, and I know that yes we are part of this universe, we are in this universe, but perhaps more important than both of those facts is that the universe is in us. When I reflect on that fact, I look up, many people feel small, cause their small and the universe is big. But I feel big because my atoms came from those stars."

— Neil deGrasse Tyson

About The Author

California girl Melina Farahmand is a storyteller at heart, an American activist, writer, and video editor. She founded Past Present Future Co. at just twelve years old, with the original purpose of empowering all women. Over the past few years, her goals have expanded exponentially, adding sustainability/protecting the environment, science, and more topics of importance to the table. In 2018, as a high school student, she published her debut book "*From Dust to Breath*," and in the

summer of 2019, an updated edition was released,
"*From Dust to Breath: Finding Our Place in the
Circle of Life.*" The new version of the book
would become number one in new releases in
Amazon's "ethics" section. Aside from running
PPF and being a student, Melina is also the Social
Media Manager and Director of Marketing for an
LA-based production company whose mission is
to create films on issues that matter by highlighting
change-makers around the globe.

Melina believes in the strength of ordinary people
coming together to do extraordinary things to
transform the world for the better for all who walk
this Earth.

Acknowledgments

To my parents, for your continued support for
my crazy dreams. You two are the best of the
best, and I love you dearly.

To my writing mentor, Rob Miller, for
inspiring me to reach for the stars and always
believing in me. Thank you for helping
me sprinkle more magic into this book. I
wouldn't have been able to finish this project
without your guidance.

To my extraordinary friend, Marilyn Foley,
you are solid gold. You've always held a very
special place in my heart, and I'm grateful
to have met you all those years ago. Thank
you for providing me with honest input,
whether on the writing or the book design. I
appreciate it more than you know.

To my amazing illustrators:

Alyssa Neumann— your beautiful pieces were truly out of this world (pun fully intended). You were an absolute joy to work with, and it's a privilege to call you my friend.

—@its_alliis

Yasmin Atienza— The moment I found your Instagram account, I knew right then and there that I wanted you to be a part of this project. Thank you for going above and beyond with every illustration you created. I loved working with you.

—@friday_concepts

To my talented book designer, Anamaria Stefan, thank you for bringing the whole vision to life.

—@ancustefan

www.ingramcontent.com/pod-product-compliance
Lightning Source LLC
LaVergne TN
LVHW010306070426
835509LV00024B/3482